simply romantic®

Tips to romance your Wife

Foreword by **Dennis Rainey**

FAMILYLIFE Publishing

FamilyLife Publishing
Little Rock, Arkansas

Simply Romantic® Tips to Romance Your Wife
© 2005 by FamilyLife Publishing
All rights reserved. Published 2005
Printed in the United States of America

11 10 09 08 07 06 05   1 2 3 4 5 6 7

ISBN: 1-57229-719-0

Written and Edited by: Margie Clark, Amy Bradford, Gregg Stutts, Mary Larmoyeux, and Dale Walters
Graphic Designer: Lee Smith
Illustration: Whitney Eoff
Cover Photography: Willie Allen

FamilyLife
Dennis Rainey, President
5800 Ranch Drive
Little Rock, Arkansas 72223
(501) 223-8663 • www.familylife.com

Contents

Foreword by Dennis Rainey .... **v**

Tips to Romance Your Wife

Romantic Messages **1**

Romantic Touch **17**

Romantic Gifts **29**

Romantic Moments **45**

Romantic Moves **61**

Romantic Advice **77**

Romantic Holidays and Special Days **93**

Acknowledgments **104**

Appendix **105**

Foreword

Most men need some inspiration to spark romance—*Simply Romantic®
Tips to Romance Your Wife* is packed with inspiring ideas to help
ordinary guys express love in extraordinary ways.

Barbara likes to remember the time when I surprised her with a trip to New
England. Although that particular event took a lot of planning, expressing love
can be as easy as tucking a short note inside her favorite magazine.

May I encourage you to take time to show your sweetheart that you care.
By using this little book to affirm your love, she will be encouraged … your
friendship will deepen … and romance will blossom.

Dennis Rainey

Dennis Rainey
President, FamilyLife

Romantic Messages

Give your wife a small journal for recording her secret romantic wishes. Read it regularly … and then make her wishes come true.

Using dry-erase markers,
leave a note to your sweetie on the bathroom mirror.

2

Using Post-it® notes all around the house,
list the reasons why you love your wife.
Hide some of them in places where
it might take days for her to find.

simply romantic

Record a love message and some of her favorite love songs
and leave it in the CD player of her car.

Call your wife on the phone and in a whisper tell her all of
the places you'd like to kiss her the next time you see her.

Send your sweetie a subtle, but suggestive, e-mail or text message.

The next time you and your wife have to be apart, leave a note for her to open each day.

Sneak a note into her vehicle that reads,
"You have me all revved up!
Put the car in gear and race on over to (location)
so I can check your fluids."

Write out your wedding vows on a small card and sign your name to them. Put the card somewhere where she will see it everyday.

simply romantic

Make a list of all the things your sweetheart does for you that
you probably take for granted. Thank her for each one.

10

Compliment your wife in front of others—especially your kids.
You may be the only one in her life who's doing it!

Leave a love note for your loved one on the toilet paper roll—
a ballpoint pen works best.

Send your wife an invitation to a night of romance in an envelope with a postmark from Romance, Arkansas 72136.

13

Scour the Internet for the perfect romantic e-card.
Send it to your wife when she least expects it.

Tell your wife you love her every morning and every night.

15

Romantic Touch

Pamper her little piggies with a pedicure—administered by you.
You will need a basin of warm water with bubbles, some candles,
and a pedicure set (available at most discount stores).

simply romantic

Celebrate Bubble Bath Night once a month with your wife.
Light candles, prepare a bath, warm a towel,
serve her favorite beverage, and then wash her.

Hold her hand whenever you are in public together.

Caress her hands as you give her a hand massage.
Express appreciation for the various things she does
with hands that show love and care for others.

Sign up as a couple for dancing lessons—let her choose the style: ballroom, swing, square dance, etc.

A woman's ears are very sensitive.
Spend time nuzzling her neck and ears.

Play the "Touching Game." Make 10 cards describing "Ways to Touch," and 10 cards with "Places to Touch" (one idea per card). Without looking, pull one card from each pile and then take action!

Play footsie with her the next time
you are having dinner at your in-laws.

33

Snuggle (just snuggle!) in bed and tell her
all the things you admire about her.

The next time you're sitting with your wife in church,
reach out and put your arm around her.

25

When you see your wife after work, kiss her.
Not just a peck on the cheek. Really kiss her.

Make foreplay the focus. Take your time.
Focus on her: Play with her hair, caress her face,
and gently stroke her arms and legs. Let things build slowly.

Romantic Gifts

Make a stop on your way home from work and pick up
that special treat your wife just loves.

Leave one of your wife's dress shoes in the front seat of the car.
Tuck a note inside, telling her that she is your Cinderella
and that she is to meet you at a certain time and
place so you can buy her a new pair of shoes.

Plan a romantic weekend at a bed-and-breakfast.
Make all of the arrangements yourself.

Start filling up a jar with your loose change.
Let your wife know that when the jar is full, you will
redeem the change for a gift card from her favorite store.

31

Ask your wife what animal you remind her of.
Purchase a stuffed version of that animal and present it to her.

Surprise her with an unexpected gift.
It doesn't have to be expensive—
just something to let her know you were thinking of her.

If your wife is a collector of figurines, tea cups, etc.,
buy her something that adds to her collection.

Take $10 to the Dollar Store and buy her 10 fun gifts that remind you of her. Over dinner, give them to her one at a time and tell her why you bought each item.

Let her purchase what she considers sexy pajamas.
Plan a special night for the fashion show.

When your wife comments on something
she would really like to have, make a note of it
and purchase it for her at Christmas (see Appendix).

Wrap up a skeleton key in a box with a note that says,
"You hold the key to my heart."

38

Secretly buy her tickets to a special event (concert, game, exhibit).
Plan a lunch or dinner date on the day of the event.
After dessert, give her the tickets.

Present her with a special piece of jewelry.
Make it even more personal by having a message engraved.

Get tickets for two (and that includes you)
to a "chick flick" she wants to see.

41

Play "Let's Make a Deal." Buy her three gifts and wrap them separately. Let her choose which one to open. Have fun trying to change her mind. Put the other two away for later.

Romantic Moments

Create your own romantic drive-in movie experience.
Drive to a remote location. Set up a portable DVD player in
the front seat of the car while you and your wife snuggle
in the back seat enjoying the snacks you brought along.

Turn your bedroom into a romantic getaway: rose petals, scented candles, and soft music. Then romance your lover.

Remember how much you talked when you were dating? How polite you were? Try that for one week and watch what happens.

Feed your wife the chocolate-covered strawberries that you made yourself. Wash and dry the strawberries and dip them in melted chocolate chips.

Remember what makes your wife laugh and then tickle her "funny bone." Laughter makes any day better.

simply romantic

Rent a convertible one weekend just for the fun of it.
Drive her to her favorite places.

Enjoy a 2nd, 3rd, or 4th honeymoon. Make reservations to spend the night at a nice hotel in your area. If money is tight, start saving $5 or $10 per week until you have enough.

Circle a day on the calendar and take your wife on a mystery date.
As the day gets closer leave her clues:
what to wear, when to be ready, etc. Keep it a surprise.

50

Over coffee ask your wife, "What are the three most romantic times we've had together?" Remember what they are and make plans to do them again.

simply romantic

Bathe the kids. Clean the kitchen. Fold the laundry. Make the bed.
Do whatever it is she normally does. Tell her to relax.

It's Christmas in July—hang a stocking with a lacy garter belt
and fill it with goodies (e.g., whipped cream, chocolate syrup).
Offer yourself as a tasty treat.

53

Find the book your wife is reading and leave some
encouraging notes in it every 20 pages or so.

54

Take her on a date to a bookstore.
Tell her you'd like to find a book you can read together.
Suggestion: *Rekindling the Romance* by Dennis and Barbara Rainey.

simply romantic

Do something together: Take a class, play tennis, start a
walking program, remodel a room, or plant a vegetable garden.
Just do it together.

What kinds of games does your wife like to play?
Cards? Board games? Sports? Play her favorite one.

simply romantic

Late one night grab a blanket and your wife and head outdoors.
Find a nice spot to lie back and look at the stars together.

58

Romantic Moves

Arrange for a babysitter and then whisk your wife away
on a special day filled with fun things she enjoys.

On those chilly mornings go out and warm up her car.
Now *that's* romantic!

60

Take an afternoon off and catch a matinee. Sit in the back row.

You probably already know, but find out your lover's
least favorite chore—and then do it for her for a month.

62

Create your own little "free cuddles" coupon book. Every time she wants to cuddle, she turns in a coupon (with no expiration date).

Tell your wife you'd like to start eating healthier so that
you'll both be around to enjoy each other longer.

64

Ask her what she enjoys in bed. Do it regularly.

simply romantic

Develop a special sign or secret word
just for her that communicates your love.

Fantasize about your wife, and then tell her what you were thinking.

simply romantic

Take some time out of your busy schedule to cook your wife a meal. Serve the meal by candlelight using your wedding china.

Leave roses in the front seat of her vehicle—just because.

69

Put your wife to bed ... tuck her in ...
tell her a story (make it a romantic story).

70

Wash her car. Be sure to vacuum it, too.

71

Treat your wife to a horse-drawn carriage ride.

Get into the habit of buying her silly
souvenirs when you're out on a date.
Purchase (or make) a special box
where she can store her keepsakes.

Romantic Advice

It takes your wife's body longer than yours to become aroused—
so don't skip the foreplay.

simply romantic

Practice good hygiene. Brush your teeth, take a shower,
and put on clean clothes before you romance your sweetie.

Remain faithful to your wife in your heart,
in your mind, and in your actions.

Good manners and chivalry are romantic.

Be a student of your spouse. Find out what she likes and dislikes, her strengths and weaknesses, and her fears.

Women view romance differently from men.
Ask your wife to describe what's romantic to her.
Don't be surprised when her ideas
sound very different from yours.

Remember your wife is God's gift to *you*.
Thank Him for her, then tell her you did so.

Plan a vacation together—in ink.

Look in her eyes and just listen.

Arrange a date with your wife at least once a month. Mark it on your calendar and take the initiative to make it happen!

83

Tell her you would marry her all over again.

84

Ask your wife to write down three things she'd like you to start doing, three things she'd like you to stop doing, and three things she'd like you to keep doing. Read the list and do it.

The next time your favorite team (or show) is on TV, skip it and take her shopping or out to dinner. Let her know that she is more important than what you're giving up.

To strengthen your marriage,
make plans to attend a Weekend to Remember seminar.
For a schedule of events visit www.familylife.com.

Write down anniversaries, special days, sizes, etc. (see Appendix).

88

simply romantic

Romantic Holidays and Special Days

Be resolute in romancing your love all year long.
Choose your favorite ideas from this little book and enter
them into your day planner, January through December.

On Valentine's Day, stage a progressive dinner
and serve each course in a different room.
End the evening with dessert in the bedroom!

March 17 is St. Patrick's Day. Celebrate it by leaving your wife
a note that says, "I'm lucky to have you by my side."

Make memories on Memorial Day. Purchase a disposable camera and then fill it up with snapshots of you and your spouse—together. You might need to ask others to take the pictures.

92

Celebrate summer by taking advantage of the longest day of the year. Start with breakfast in bed, treat her to lunch, then end the day with a summertime barbeque for two.

This Fourth of July, light up your own fireworks in the night sky. Add glow-in-the-dark stars to your bedroom ceiling— and snuggle under your own private starry sky.

Each day in the month of August leave her a Hershey's kiss where she'll be sure to find it. Ask her to save the paper flags in a jar and redeem them for actual kisses.

As the days begin to turn chilly, take your "pumpkin" to the pumpkin patch. Let her choose a few to accent your front door. Bring along a Thermos of hot apple cider to share.

On the third Saturday in October buy your sweetheart
a few fall treats for Sweetest Day:
popcorn balls, caramel apples, and candy corn, to name a few.

Don't be a turkey this Thanksgiving—help your wife in the kitchen!
And don't forget to tell her why you're thankful for her.

98

On Christmas Eve give your little "Santa" a basket full of bubble bath supplies and then get the water ready for her.

simply romantic

Acknowledgments

We want to thank the following people for their contributions to
TIPS to Romance Your Wife:

FamilyLife staff and visitors to www.familylife.com,
Sabrina Beasley, Amy Bradford, Margie Clark, Eric Dahinden,
Hugh Duncan, Dan Gaffney, Marcie Hefner, Kathy Harrill,
Sharon Hill, Nicole Kinzler, Phil Krause, Cindy Landes,
Mary Larmoyeux, Marla Livers, Julie Majors, Todd Nagel,
Jenni Smith, Lee Smith, John Stokes, Gregg Stutts, Suzanne
Thomas, Denise Truelove, and Dale Walters.

Appendix

Sizes for Her:

Jeans: _____

Dress: _____

Shirt: _____

Shoes: _____

Ring: _____

Other: _____

_____

simply romantic

Gift list:

_____

_____

_____

_____

_____

_____

_____